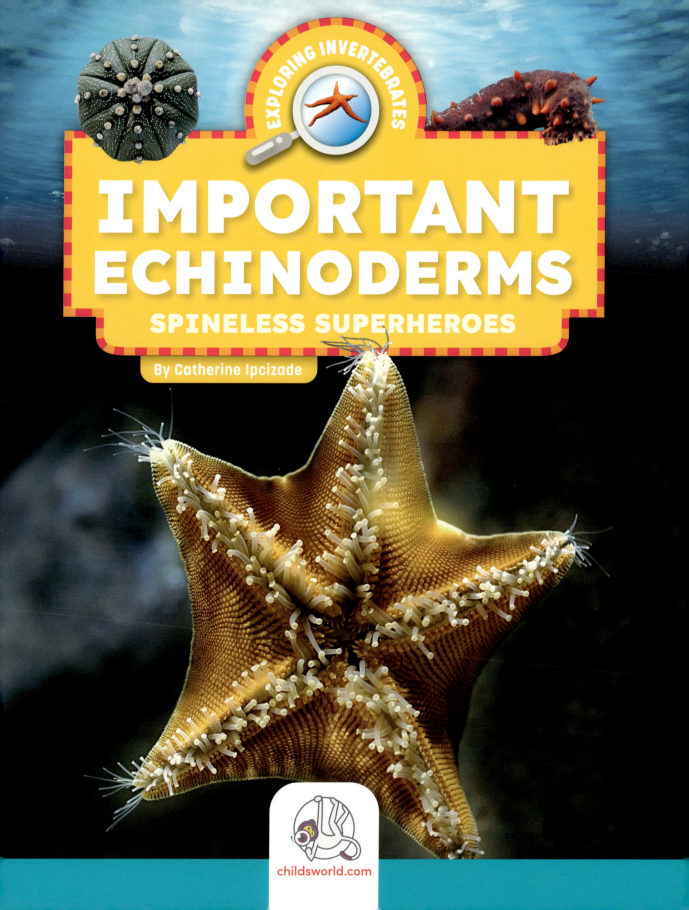

**Published by The Child's World®**
800-599-READ • childsworld.com

**Copyright © 2025 by The Child's World®**
All rights reserved. No part of this book may be reproduced or utilized in any form or by any means without written permission from the publisher.

**Photography Credits**
Cover: ©Paul Starosta/Stone/Getty Images; ©Science Artwork/Science Photo Library/Getty Images; ©Adam Ke/Shutterstock; ©g images.com/Shutterstock; ©Romolo Tavani/Shutterstock; ©JAKKAPAN PRAMMANASIK/Moment Open/Getty Images; page 3, 6–7: ©Damsea/Shutterstock; page 4–5: ©Abstract Aerial Art/Difital Vision/Getty Images; page 5, 7, 23: ©Bennewitz/E+/Getty Images; page 5: ©tamara_kulikova/iStock/Getty Images; page 5, 24; ©Flaming Pumpkin/E+/Getty Images; page 5: ©imagenavi/Getty Images; ©Alex Bramwell/Moment/Getty Images; page 6–7: ©Damsea/Shutterstock; page 7: ©Glasshouse Images/The Image Bank/Getty Images; page 9: ©Damocean/iStock/Getty Images; ©grayjay/Getty Images; page 10–11: ©Michael Ziegler/E+/Getty Images; page 12: ©Romolo Tavani/Shutterstock; page 13: ©Aleksei Permiakov/Moment/Getty Images; ©Hal Beral/Corbis/Getty Images; page 14-15: ©Dee-Ann Cranston/iStock/Getty Images; page 15: ©Wikimedia Commons; page 16–17: ©Stuart Westmorland/Corbis Documentary/Getty Images; page 18: ©Walter Geiersperger/Corbis Documentary/Getty Images; ©page 20: ©Thomas Jackson/iStock/Getty Images; page 21: ©Christina Felschen/Moment/Getty Images; page 22: ©Lori Bye

**ISBN Information**
9781503894525 (Reinforced Library Binding)
9781503894792 (Portable Document Format)
9781503895614 (Online Multi-user eBook)
9781503896437 (Electronic Publication)

**LCCN**
2024941435

**Printed in the United States of America**

## ABOUT THE AUTHOR

**Catherine Ipcizade** is a college professor and the author of more than 30 books for children. She loves photography, cooking, and spending time with her family in sunny California and the mountains of Utah. Her favorite word is "serendipity" because life is full of unexpected, fortunate surprises.

# CONTENTS

**CHAPTER 1**
## MEET THE ECHINODERMS . . . 4

**CHAPTER 2**
## A CLOSER LOOK . . . 8

**CHAPTER 3**
## LIFE CYCLE . . . 12

**CHAPTER 4**
## ECHINODERMS IN THE WORLD . . . 16

**CHAPTER 5**
## KEEPING ECHINODERMS SAFE . . . 20

Wonder More . . . 21
Let's Make a Sea Star! . . . 22
Glossary . . . 23
Find Out More . . . 24
Index . . . 24

# CHAPTER 1
# MEET THE ECHINODERMS

A purple sand dollar washes up on shore. It lies on its back wiggling hundreds of tiny spines in the air. The sand dollar is alive. It needs to be turned over so it can wash back out to sea. Sand dollars are echinoderms (eh-KY-nuh-dermz).

Echinoderms are the spiny creatures of the ocean. They are invertebrates. That means they do not have backbones. Instead, echinoderms have a tough, spiny cover to protect them. Many echinoderms have hundreds of legs. They are sometimes called tube legs or tube feet. These limbs have suction cups at the ends. This is how echinoderms attach themselves to rocks and other ocean surfaces.

Echinoderms come in all shapes and sizes. Sea stars usually have five arms. Sea cucumbers are long and bumpy like a cucumber. Sea urchins are spiky all over. Sand dollars are flat. Pea urchins are smaller than a dime, while a sunflower sea star's width can be up to three feet (0.9 m). That's about the length of a guitar! All echinoderms have one thing in common—they have mouths on the underside of their bodies.

Echinoderms live in oceans all over the world. Most echinoderms, such as sea urchins, sea stars, and sand dollars, live in shallow water. Some live in **tide pools** next to the ocean. Sea stars like to eat clams, mussels, oysters, or shellfish. Sea urchins feed on algae and seaweed.

Other echinoderms live deeper in the ocean. Brittle stars sweep their arms through the sand to grab small worms and tiny fish. Sea cucumbers use sticky **tentacles** to pick up dead and **decaying** matter on the ocean floor. Sea lilies use feather-like arms to sweep up tiny sea creatures as they float by in the water.

Although some sea urchins do not have spines, most are covered in colorful spikes.

## LET'S TAKE A LOOK!

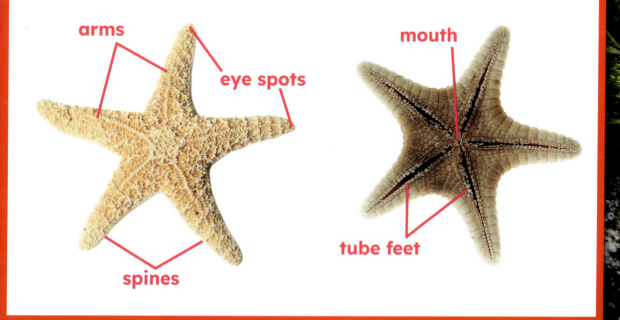

- arms
- eye spots
- spines
- mouth
- tube feet

# A CLOSER LOOK

A brittle star hides under a rock. One of its arms is sticking out. A hungry fish comes by. Chomp! It eats the brittle star's arm. Not to worry—soon, the brittle star will grow a new arm.

The ability to regrow a limb is called **regeneration**. It is one of the things that makes echinoderms different from many other creatures. When an echinoderm loses a limb, its **stem cells** take over. They multiply and soon create a new limb. Sea stars often regenerate when they lose an arm. Sometimes, the lost arm grows into a whole new sea star!

# SEA STAR LIMB REGENERATION

Sea stars can be many different colors. Some are bright red, orange, or pink. Others are blue, purple, green, and even brown or white.

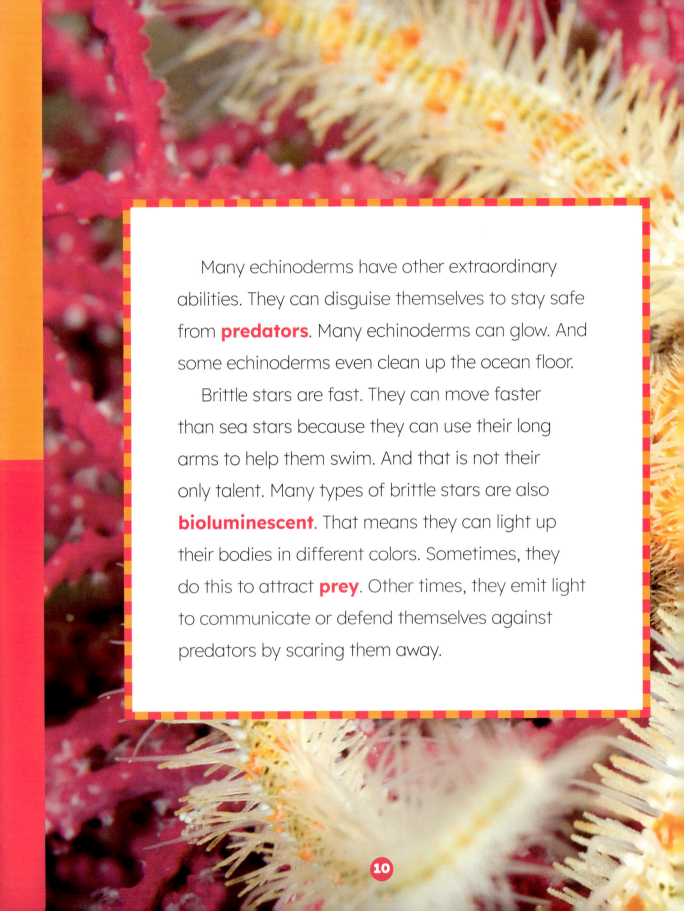

Many echinoderms have other extraordinary abilities. They can disguise themselves to stay safe from **predators**. Many echinoderms can glow. And some echinoderms even clean up the ocean floor.

Brittle stars are fast. They can move faster than sea stars because they can use their long arms to help them swim. And that is not their only talent. Many types of brittle stars are also **bioluminescent**. That means they can light up their bodies in different colors. Sometimes, they do this to attract **prey**. Other times, they emit light to communicate or defend themselves against predators by scaring them away.

### NO SAND DOLLARS HERE

Sand dollars are masters of disguise! Their flat bodies make it easy for them to bury themselves in the sand. This hides the star pattern on their top shell, which makes them easy to spot. The sand protects them from predators. It also helps sand dollars find food. Sand dollars use the spines that cover their bodies to help them move and find food particles in the sand.

Brittle stars have long, whip-like arms that can grow up to almost 24 inches (60 cm) long.

# CHAPTER 3

# LIFE CYCLE

Some echinoderms have a few babies at a time. But many echinoderms push out millions of eggs into the water at one time. Because eggs are vulnerable to predators, only a few may survive. But some find safety and grow into adults. Echinoderms can live up to 10 years.

Echinoderms spend most of their time finding food and avoiding predators. They may live near other echinoderms, but they usually do not work together to hunt or survive. However, they do live in **symbiosis** with other creatures, including emperor shrimp. The shrimp might hitch a ride on the back of a sea cucumber. This helps the shrimp avoid predators. Emperor shrimp also eat **parasites** that can make sea cucumbers sick.

Since sea cucumbers can be several feet long, they can provide transportation for many emperor shrimp at one time.

Emperor shrimp feed on the parasites and decaying material often found on a sea cucumber's skin.

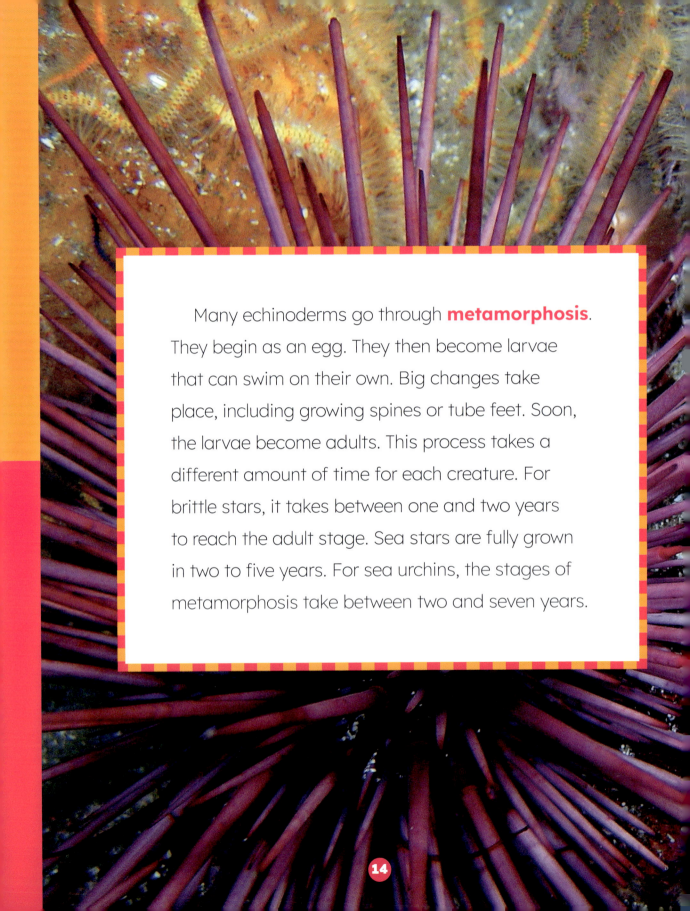

Many echinoderms go through **metamorphosis**. They begin as an egg. They then become larvae that can swim on their own. Big changes take place, including growing spines or tube feet. Soon, the larvae become adults. This process takes a different amount of time for each creature. For brittle stars, it takes between one and two years to reach the adult stage. Sea stars are fully grown in two to five years. For sea urchins, the stages of metamorphosis take between two and seven years.

## LIFE CYCLE OF A SEA URCHIN

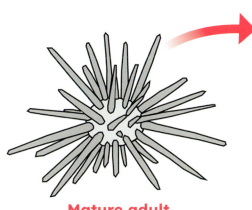
**Mature adult**

**Egg**

**Embryo**

**Larva**

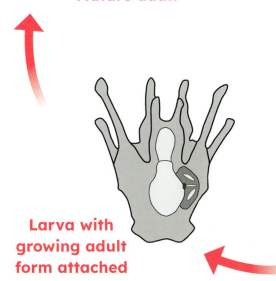
**Larva with growing adult form attached**

# CHAPTER 4
# ECHINODERMS IN THE WORLD

Echinoderms are the ocean's clean-up crew. They help to keep the ocean clean. When sea stars eat clams, mussels, and shellfish, they help prevent overpopulation. Overpopulation occurs when there are extremely large numbers of animals. Sea cucumbers are like vacuum cleaners. They help the ocean by sucking up dead and decaying matter from the ocean floor.

A sea star opens shellfish with its tube feet. Then, the sea star's stomach comes out of its mouth like a tongue and eats the shellfish.

## SYMBOLIC SEA STARS

Sea stars are symbols in many cultures. The fact that sea stars can regenerate an arm makes them a symbol of rebirth or starting over. They are given as gifts or placed in homes. They remind people that they, too, can renew themselves after a difficult time.

Scientists have discovered sea lily fossils that date back before the age of dinosaurs.

Echinoderm **fossils** are important for research. Scientists study echinoderm fossils to learn about their **evolution**. This helps researchers to better understand how some animals change over time. It also helps them to understand how different kinds of animals interacted with one another long ago. The oldest echinoderm fossil is 540 million years old. These fossils are preserved well because echinoderms have a hard skeleton. The fossils are often found in **sedimentary** rocks. These fossils can also help researchers determine how old a rock is!

## CHAPTER 5

# KEEPING ECHINODERMS SAFE

People often enjoy finding echinoderms in tide pools. Because sea stars and other echinoderms are found in shallow waters, people like to pick them up. But holding echinoderms is not a good idea. The echinoderm can be harmed. And even though an echinoderm might regenerate a new limb, that process takes time. People can protect these important ocean creatures by admiring them from a distance or handling them with care in aquariums or science centers.

# WONDER MORE

### Wondering About New Information
What new information did you learn about echinoderms? Write down two facts that surprised you.

### Wondering How It Matters
Sea stars eat clams, mussels, and shellfish. Why is this important? What would happen to oceans if sea stars did not eat these creatures?

### Wondering Why
Why do you think living alone is important for most echinoderms?

### Ways to Keep Wondering
After reading this book, what questions do you have about echinoderms? Which echinoderms would you like to learn more about? What can you do to learn more about them?

# LET'S MAKE A SEA STAR!

Sea stars are like jewels in a tide pool. Let's make one!

### Steps to Take

1) On your paper, draw a sea star with five arms.

2) Use your scissors to cut out the sea star.

3) Paint the sea star any color you'd like! You might even paint each arm a different color!

4) Use glitter and add googly eyes to finish your sea star.

### Supplies
- paper
- scissors
- pencil
- glue stick
- paint
- paintbrush
- glitter
- googly eyes

# GLOSSARY

**bioluminescent** (by-oh-loom-ih-NES-ent) Something that is bioluminescent glows.

**decaying** (dee-KAY-ing) Decaying means rotting.

**evolution** (ev-uh-LOO-shun) Evolution is the change in a species over a long period of time.

**fossils** (FAH-suls) Fossils are the remains of plants and animals that lived long ago.

**metamorphosis** (met-uh-MOR-fuh-sis) Metamorphosis is the process of growing from a baby to adult in animals.

**parasites** (PAYR-uh-sytz) Parasites are animals that live in or on another living thing, called a host.

**predators** (PRED-uh-turz) Predators are creatures that get food by killing and consuming other organisms.

**prey** (PRAY) Prey is an animal that is hunted for food.

**regeneration** (ree-gen-er-AY-shun) Regeneration occurs when echinoderms lose a limb, like an arm, and grow a new one in its place.

**sedimentary** (se-di-MEN-tuh-ree) Sedimentary rocks are rocks formed from other rocks or once-living organisms.

**stem cells** (STEM CELS) Stem cells are cells in an organism that can turn into any other kind of cells.

**symbiosis** (sim-bee-OH-sis) Symbiosis occurs when two organisms live in harmony with one another and help each other survive.

**tentacles** (TEN-tuh-kuls) Tentacles are thin structures around the head of an animal or insect used for feeling or grasping.

**tide pools** (TIDE POOLS) Tide pools are small areas of salt water that form in the sand around the ocean.

## FIND OUT MORE

### In the Library

Brundle, Joanna. *Echinoderms.* New York, NY: KidHaven Publishing, 2020.

Emminizer, Theresa. *What if Sea Urchins Disappeared?* New York, NY: Gareth Stevens, 2020.

Zimmerman, Adaline J. *Sea Stars.* Minneapolis, MN: Pogo Books, 2022.

### On the Web

Visit our website for links about echinoderms:
**childsworld.com/links**

*Note to Parents, Caregivers, Teachers, and Librarians: We routinely verify our web links to make sure they are safe and active sites. So encourage your readers to check them out!*

## INDEX

arms, 6–8, 10–11, 22

brittle stars 5–6, 8, 10–11, 14

decaying matter 6, 16

eggs 12, 14–15

food 11–12
fossil 18–19

regeneration 8–9

sand dollar 4–6, 11
sea cucumber 5–6, 12–13, 16
sea star 5–6, 9–10, 14, 16–17
sea urchin 5–7, 14–15
spines 4, 7, 11, 14

tide pool 6, 20
tube feet 4, 7, 14, 16